IMAGES FROM SCIENCE

An Exhibition of Scientific Photography

IMAGES FROM SCIENCE

An Exhibition of Scientific Photography

Organized by the School of Photographic Arts and Sciences

ROCHESTER INSTITUTE OF TECHNOLOGY

CARY GRAPHIC ARTS PRESS

2002

Images from Science: An Exhibition of Scientific Photography
http://images.rit.edu/

Produced for Rochester Institute of Technology by Cary Graphic Arts Press.

Melbert B. Cary, Jr. Graphic Arts Collection
Rochester Institute of Technology
90 Lomb Memorial Drive
Rochester, New York 14623-5604

Telephone: 585.475.6766

Fax: 585.475.6900

Internet: *http://wally.rit.edu/cary/carypress.html*

Library of Congress Cataloging-in-Publication Data

Images from science : an exhibition of scientific photography /
Sponsored by School of Photographic Arts and Sciences, Rochester
Institute of Technology.
        p. cm.
Summary: The catalog of a photography exhibition held at Rochester
Institute of Technology in the fall of 2002, featuring photographs and
explanatory captions from photographers in all scientific disciplines.
    ISBN 0-9713459-9-6 (pbk.)
  1. Photography--Scientific applications--Exhibitions. [1.
Photography--Scientific applications.] I. Rochester Institute of
Technology. School of Photographic Arts and Sciences.
    TR692 .I433 2002
    779´.95´07474789--dc21
                                        2002007262

OVERLEAF: Lennart Nilsson, Sweden. *Scandianthus costatus.* Photomicrograph, 1980. This rare fossilized bud of *Scandianthus costatus*—one of the earliest plants to appear on dry land—is magnified 230 times. A possible ancestor of present-day ferns, it is estimated that *Scandianthus* became extinct 78 million years ago. The scanning electron photomicrograph reveals that the flower's surface is ribbed and covered with small openings. The tips of the petals are also apparent. The photograph was colorized subsequent to its making. Courtesy of the photographer, Karolinska Institute, Stockholm, Sweden.

COVER: Kathleen McCarthy and Matthew H. Smith, United States. *Polarized Landscape #4, New York.* Composite digital photograph, 2002. Courtesy of the photographers.

Printed in Hong Kong through InterPress Ltd.

ISBN 0-9713459-9-6

TABLE OF CONTENTS

P HOTOGRAPHY COURSES WERE FIRST OFFERED at the Rochester Institute of Technology in 1902. The production of the *Images from Science* project is a fitting tribute to 100 years of photographic activities in this university. The School of Photographic Arts and Sciences has a rich history of contributions to photographic education and exploration. This project is one more example of many significant achievements that have come out of the school and its faculty. The imagination that led to *Images from Science* could only have come from individuals who are committed to excellence in photographic art and science. RIT, and the College of Imaging Arts and Sciences in particular, are proud to be associated with the important and beautiful work represented on the pages that follow. On behalf of the university, I thank Professor Andrew Davidhazy and Professor Michael Peres for their impressive achievement.

DR. JOAN STONE
Dean, College of Imaging Arts and Sciences
Rochester Institute of Technology

S ILVER HALIDE PHOTOGRAPHY, invented in 1839, depicts scenes and subjects with a precision that drawing cannot approach. Soon after photography's invention, scientists, researchers, and physicians began using it to document and share certain aspects of their work, and they have continued to do so ever since. Their images, usually created in laboratories far removed from the eye of the general public, have seldom won the wide recognition and acceptance accorded other photographic genres. Though a few scientific photographers—Eadweard Muybridge (1867–1904), Dr. Harold Edgerton (1903–1990), and Lennart Nilsson (b. 1922) among them—have won some measure of fame among admirers of photography, most remain unrecognized outside the circle of their immediate peers.

Images from Science has been created to promote a wider appreciation of scientific photography by showcasing beautiful, data-rich, but rarely seen images drawn from oceanography, geology, biology, engineering, medicine, and physics. We first conceived the idea in spring 2001 during a casual conversation over coffee. By mid-summer 2001 we had determined that the project would comprise three major components: a photographic exhibition at Rochester Institute of Technology, a related Web gallery, and a four-color printed catalogue—all budgeted at $17,000, none of which was in hand.

We chose the Internet as our principal promotional tool, hoping that it would provide an efficient, low-cost means of attracting the worldwide interest and participation we sorely wanted but were hardly assured of getting. Our Web site described the project this way:

> Organized to showcase photographs made in pursuit of science, *IMAGES from SCIENCE* welcomes pictures made with any imaging tools as the source, not only traditional photographic ones. This invitation, the exhibition's promotion and image contribution, etc., will primarily be conducted relying on the Internet. We would appreciate you sharing this announcement with others to accomplish our goal of developing this international exhibition.

> Acceptance into this juried show will be based on the photograph's impact, the image's aesthetics, the degree of difficulty in the making of the photograph, as well as other related criteria. A maximum of four images may be submitted for judging. JPEG files with a resolution of about 640 x 480 pixels (or equivalent) should be mailed to *RITphoto@rit.edu* by March 30, 2002.

A frighteningly small trickle of submissions began arriving in August 2001, and by the end of November a mere three photographers had submitted less than a dozen images in all. Faced with the real prospect of humiliation, we worked hard during RIT's January 2002 recess to spread the word about the project.

A flurry of responses began arriving around February 20. In the week before the judging deadline, nearly 60 photographers submitted a total of some 180 pictures. Between then and February 27 another 23 entries were submitted, by which time the exhibition's computer account was swamped by the deluge of image data. When the final tally was in, 87 photographers representing 14 countries had submitted more than 290 pictures for consideration.

Judges were invited at various stages of the project. Dr. David Malin, having agreed to write the guest essay for the catalogue, rightly argued that an international project required international judges. Lacking funds to support travel, we again turned to the Internet, developing a judges' Web site complete with all entries and support materials. Judges were selected to represent a wide range of attitudes about pictures and were ultimately drawn from the ranks of scientists, scientific photographers, educators, practicing artists, and photographic editors. Most of them represented organizations whose indirect involvement lent additional prestige and validity to our project. Each judge received the following instructions:

VOTE FOR 75 IMAGES.

This number of votes, multiplied by the seven judges, should create enough overall "voting balance" to allow the selection of approximately 50 of the best images. We would like to have no more than two entries per person, if possible. This is important for the project to establish a large, diverse book/exhibition. If in the judging outcomes, one individual(s) exceeds more than two selections, the project coordinators will eliminate the photograph with the least votes.

SELECT ONE ENTRY FOR GUARANTEED SELECTION.

The organizers want to provide a curatorial opportunity for each judge to select an image for automatic inclusion in the exhibition. After making this selection, please provide us a short written description of why you made this choice.

Fifty-eight photographs were ultimately chosen for inclusion.

As we complete the production of this catalogue, we have seen our simple idea become something far greater than we anticipated. We congratulate our new colleagues whose aesthetic and scientific achievements made this exhibition and catalogue possible, and thank them for trusting us with their images.

Our title-page image, Lennart Nilsson's picture of the 78-million-year-old flower fossil, was chosen in tribute to Nilsson's importance as a scientific photographer and his lifelong dedication to producing images of a sort that can only be made by those who combine deep scientific knowledge with a full mastery of complex instrumentation. His work exemplifies the best that scientific photography has to offer, and serves as an ideal entry point to the field. We hope that all of those who encounter *Images from Science*—whether as an exhibition, Web site, or catalogue— will enjoy it as much as we have enjoyed producing it.

PROFESSOR MICHAEL PERES
Chair, Biomedical Photographic Communications
School of Photographic Arts and Sciences
Rochester Institute of Technology

PROFESSOR ANDREW DAVIDHAZY
Chair, Imaging and Photographic Technology
School of Photographic Arts and Sciences
Rochester Institute of Technology

THE MAKING OF IMAGES, representations of the world around us, seems to have been part of the life of our species ever since we evolved to the point of being identifiably human. One could argue that it is an enduring and distinct human characteristic to attempt to understand nature by capturing some kind of picture of it.

Thirty thousand or more years ago our ancestors left tangible evidence of this in their cave paintings. It is not surprising that no other creatures seem to create such pictures, for it requires considerable dexterity and intellect to translate a dynamic, colorful, three-dimensional scene into the static, two-dimensional, monochromatic outline typical of cave paintings. Those of us who, despite thousands of generations of evolution, have failed to develop such skill are fortunate in that we can still enjoy, interpret, and respond to these images and recreate elements of the original tableau in our mind's eye.

Many people would call ability in observation and interpretation the essence of art, but it is also the essence of scientific imagery. What differs is the motivation of the creator. The eye of the interpreter is a different matter altogether, and is an underlying theme of the *Images from Science* project.

Those of our ancestors who chose to represent some aspect of their experience on the rough surfaces of cave walls did so not from any scientific motivation, but from a desire—one much like that of today's artists and photographers—to record something of the world in which they lived. Nonetheless, their dramatic pictures are scientifically useful because they reveal information about long-gone events, environments, cultures and traditions. The artistry of these pictures cannot be ignored, but it is their improbable existence that perhaps most captures the imagination. Their information content, which may not reveal itself at first glance, comes as a welcome bonus.

Objectivity is the most important requirement of illustration claiming to represent some aspect of science, but illustration is not an objective business. The choice of the method, and the moment of creation will always leave something of the creator's stamp on a picture. The mere selections of field of view, magnification, and focus setting on a microscope inevitably reflect choices made by the microscopist before the shutter is pressed to capture the image. To be useful, the record must be presented as a print, a slide, or in any of a dozen other formats, each of which imposes a further layer of subjectivity.

Many of us see this not as a limitation of scientific illustration but as an enormous advantage. It allows us the freedom to make our pictures interesting, not only to other scientists but to members of the lay public who may be utterly indifferent to the processes of science. Astronomy is a great exemplar of this, especially the stream of exciting images emerging daily from the Hubble Space Telescope. These are mostly made from data obtained for scientific purposes, but their aesthetic appeal cannot be ignored and is actively exploited by NASA.

Astronomical images from a much earlier age, however, can tell us something about the subjective nature of scientific illustration and about the pace of events in science today.

SCIENCE FROM ART

The making of pictures in the service of science has a long history. Though we now think of images from science primarily in terms of photography or its electronic equivalent, in the days before photography much wonderful and quite beautiful work was done with pen, paint, and paper. Many examples of such work—including drawings and paintings of plants, animals, and birds, especially those found in the new worlds of the Americas and Australia—are available from all the sciences active prior to the introduction of photography (circa 1840). These images, nowadays valued more for their artistry than their scientific content, were often the sole means of conveying visual information about exotic locales in an age when travel was mostly open only to the adventurous (and occasionally unfortunate) few.

Some artist-scientists devoted endless hours to portraying not such clearly visible (if often reluctant) subjects as birds and beasts or images on the threshold of human vision. Some of these images were unseen in all but the largest telescopes of their day—distant places that, while part of the natural world, could not be visited or studied up close. The study of the stars, nebulae, and galaxies has some unique characteristics. Firstly, it is a purely observational science. Fortunately we cannot experiment with the stars; if we could, the closest star, the Sun, would be our most likely subject. Because we are currently conducting an uncontrolled experiment of uncertain outcome with the air and water of our own planet, I feel it would be foolish to trifle with that other essential ingredient of life, the energy from the Sun. Though we dispatch probes to the nearest planets, the rest of the universe is spared our direct intervention for now, so we are obliged to learn about it by looking. Nowadays we look with ever-more-sensitive instruments covering most of the electromagnetic spectrum.

It was not always so, and from the invention of the telescope in the early 1600s until about 1880, images of the objects of the night sky were laboriously studied by eye and sketched by hand. At the urging of nineteenth-century England's leading astronomer, Sir John Herschel, the Sun began being monitored daily by means of photography in 1858 or so, but the nighttime astronomical telescopes and photographic emulsions of the time could not support the long exposures needed to photograph faint celestial objects.

Herschel was knighted by the young Queen Victoria in June 1838, soon after his return from a four-year expedition to observe the southern skies from Cape Town, South Africa. While there he had made copious notes and detailed drawings of many astronomical objects, among them the famous Orion nebula.

We now know this to be the nearest star-forming region, but to Herschel and his contemporaries the Great Nebula in Orion was an enduring mystery, the most conspicuous of thousands of similar but fainter fuzzy objects between the stars. He made meticulous drawings of it with the declared purpose of providing future generations of scientists with a totally objective record of the state of the nebula and the disposition of the stars within it. Herschel hoped that later observations would show changes that might reveal the nature of this curious misty patch. He made his notes and initial sketches in 1832–33, but the results were not widely published until 1847. Fortunately he owned the telescope he used, providing him with more observation time than other colleagues.

Though Herschel was very familiar with the photographic experiments of William Henry Fox-Talbot in England, he was surprised to learn in January 1839 of Daguerre's announcement of a practical system invented in France. Within a week of hearing the news, Herschel began making his own photographs. He thereafter consistently encouraged the use of photography to record scientific results and phenomena, but his own interests were in the process rather than its applications.

Photography of the night sky remained elusive until a decade after Herschel's death in 1871. In the meantime, other drawings of the Orion nebula were made, most notably in 1860 by William Parsons, third Earl of Rosse, who was also keen to detect changes in the nebula and whose telescope was more powerful than Herschel's.

I reproduce Herschel's and Parsons's drawings [page VIII] and the differences between them are obvious. They result not from changes in the nebula or in telescopic power, but from subjective differences in the way their creators saw,

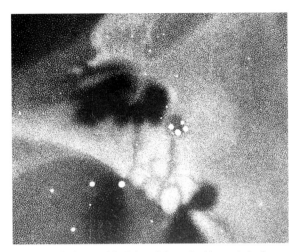

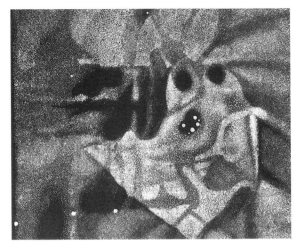

John Herschel's drawing of the Orion nebula, made with an 18-inch telescope during his period in Cape Town, South Africa, in the 1830s.

In Ireland in the 1840s, William Parsons (Lord Rosse) constructed the world's largest telescope, which he used in making this drawing of the Orion nebula.

remembered, and sketched what was essentially the same subject. The nebula has not changed significantly since Herschel saw it in the 1830s, and I include recent images of it to show that in their different ways both astronomers managed to capture the essence of its structure but not its impossibly intricate detail.

Today the difficulty of making drawings as detailed as these is hard to fully appreciate. A modern solid-state CCD camera attached to Herschel's telescope could record in seconds detail he was unable to capture in weeks of patient observation. Though the Orion nebula is among the brightest in the sky, it is still intrinsically faint. Even moonlight renders it invisible. The nebula could thus only be seen by the dark-adapted eye, and the act of lighting a candle to transfer the visual memory to paper destroyed that dark adaptation for many minutes. The drawing and telescopic image could therefore never be directly compared, unlike drawings made from microscopes, for example. This makes these images an interesting study in the subjective nature of the link between eye, memory, and sketch pad: despite both astronomers' determination to make a completely objective record, their results differ radically.

 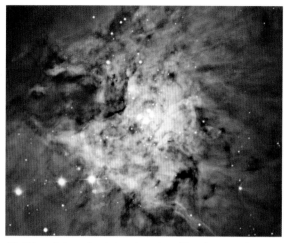

The Orion nebula, made from a three-minute exposure taken with the Anglo-Australian Telescope in 1979.

The Orion nebula, a color photograph constructed from three, one-minute exposures made with the Anglo-Australian Telescope in 1979.

All of this was to change when photography was introduced to nighttime astronomy in the 1880s, but for reasons peculiar to astronomy, drawings of the planets and the moon long remained superior to photographic representations. Now, of course, the moon has been walked upon and the planets have been visited by imaging satellites. But in ways that their authors never intended, these early drawings, like the ancient cave paintings, reveal aspects of the science of perception.

ART FROM SCIENCE

The astronomical drawings reproduced here are not particularly memorable works of art, but long before photography was invented some scientific illustrators, either by accident or design, did manage to make striking images of scientific subjects. Among the first and most enduringly notable of them was Leonardo da Vinci, whose anatomical sketches revealed a clarity of vision and understanding of purpose rare even among the physicians of the day. Vesalius' anatomical drawings are also striking representations of the human body, showing it simultaneously dissected and flayed. Both artists were driven to reproduce what they found as a result of experiment and observation. In so doing they cast aside centuries of dogma and laid the foundations of modern anatomy and of technical illustration.

The work of these pioneers has had a visual impact far beyond their practical purposes. I recall my initial shock and subsequent morbid curiosity as a child at the details of a Vesalius drawing, and I learned more about childbirth from Leonardo's famous drawing of the fetus in utero than from any euphemistic sketch in a school biology textbook. Both of these images are reproduced in that marvelous survey of scientific imagery *Beauty of Another Order,* an excellent collection of essays edited by Ann Thomas to accompany an exhibition of the same name at the National Gallery of Canada in Ottawa in 1997. It includes many other examples of pre- and post-photographic illustrations that subtly emphasize the importance of aesthetics in the making of a scientifically useful picture. Once that importance is acknowledged, it is but a short step to justify the creation of images of scientific subjects specifically intended to capture the eye. The best such images unselfconsciously achieve this end by simultaneously working on several levels and serving several purposes.

I support the idea of using such photographs as a means of self-expression. Doing so can only help any maker of scientific pictures better appreciate that such images can be enjoyed for their own sake, both by their makers and by others who may neither know nor care about the underlying science. Such artistic creativity helps the artist-scientist better understand the fuzzy regions between objective and subjective representation. More importantly, it brings scientific images into the public domain.

Once these pictures are made public, the best of them attract the curious, who tend to ask questions—most typically "What is that?" The answer to that, be it expressed as a caption or in any other form, should be direct and non-technical, and might well be as simple as "a microbe" or "a galaxy." Whatever the subject, the onlooker will leave a little wiser, and the picture will have served both a scientific and a cultural purpose.

Science is a recent way of trying to come to terms with the natural world; art is another, much older effort. Generally (though not universally) these activities are seen as separate, with little interchange of ideas between the two camps.

In our time art and science do not intersect but travel in parallel, each contained within its definition of the universe. This has been so for a long time and seems likely to remain so for some time yet, but there are signs of change.

The energetic streams carrying forward the two disciplines now seem to run in parallel, and parallel lines do not intersect. There are many bridges between them, however, and it seems that the number and carrying capacity of these bridges is increasing with time and that the links are growing stronger without appearing to deflect the separate streams beneath—all of which would seem to support my contention that art and science have shared ancient origins in one distinctly human characteristic, the wellspring of our curiosity.

It is true that art and science have diverged and now seem to lead separate lives. But as the links between them grow ever stronger, the once-empty middle ground is filling with people who recognize that science has much to contribute to the world of the artist and that aesthetic sensibilities are vital in creating and comprehending images from science.

DR. DAVID MALIN
Anglo-Australian Observatory
RMIT (Royal Melbourne Institute of Technology)

DEE BREGER

Microplankton, 2001

Scanning electron photomicrograph; x4,500 approximate magnification;
post-capture digital colorization

Lamont-Doherty Earth Observatory of Columbia University, Palisades, New York, United States

This shell detail of a single-celled marine animal called a radiolarian shows that the organism has eaten three smaller plant-like diatoms. The diatoms have been incorporated into the radiolarian's shell for additional strength.

6

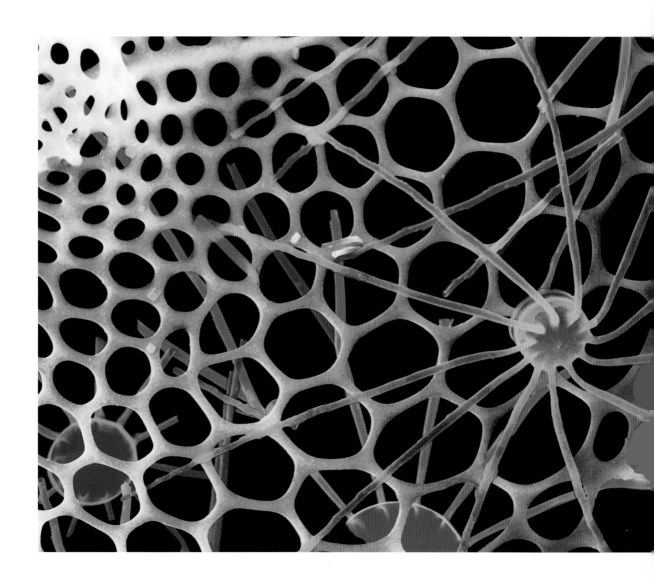

Dee Breger

Fertilization, 2001

Scanning electron photomicrograph; x4,500 approximate magnification;
post-capture digital colorization

Lamont-Doherty Earth Observatory of Columbia University, Palisades, New York, United States

A grain of pollen from goldenrod, *Solidago* sp., has just begun to grow a tube along the surface
of the flower's stigma. The genetic material is thus delivered to the ovary located far below.

9

HEIDI CARTWRIGHT

Circuit Collage, 2000

Digitally manipulated photographs

Prince of Wales Medical Research Institute, Randwick, Australia

This image was part of a 2000 exhibition entitled, "Homunculus: Who's Inside Your Brain?" that benefited the Prince of Wales Medical Research Institute. Dr. Virginia Macdonald also collaborated by contributing captions for each of the 25 images that provided an inside look into the human brain. *Circuit Collage* represents the different circuitry in the brain and the complexities involved in thought.

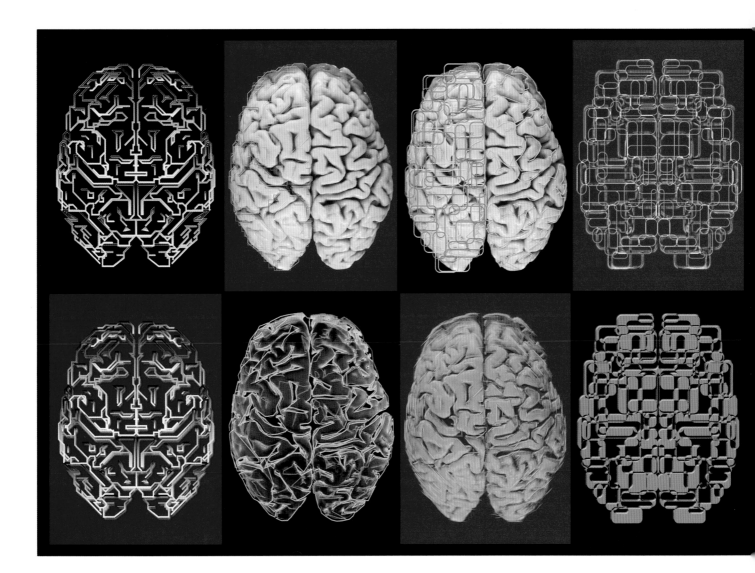

GEORGE COOK

Chironomid Larva Posterior Prolegs, 2002

Digital photomicrograph; x200 approximate magnification

Rochester, New York, United States

The study of aquatic organisms is useful in gauging water quality. Midges, or non-biting flies of the order Diptera, family Chironomidae, are common inhabitants of these environments. Chironomids are identified by examining the antennae, mouthparts, proleg claws, setae, and ventral tubules of slide-mounted specimens through light microscope examination at up to x500 magnifications.

13

Jhodie Duncan

New Wave of Life on the Sands of Time, 1999

Digital photomicrograph

University of Melbourne, Department of Anatomy and Cell Biology, Melbourne, Australia

There is a constant struggle for life in every situation. As the staining solution dried on this histological tissue section, crystals began to grow—eventually taking over the entire area. New life seemed to be represented by the whiteness of the crystals on the dark background. At the same time, other patterns were reminiscent of wave-washed sand.

Jhodie Duncan

Can't See the Forest for the Trees, 2000

Digital photomicrograph

University of Melbourne, Department of Anatomy and Cell Biology, Melbourne, Australia

Purkinje cells are neurons of the cerebellum that communicate electrical impulses through structures known as dendritic trees. Multitudes of the branching cells in this tissue section create a virtual forest. The smaller, darker-stained supportive neurons also add a visual dimension of depth and an eerie feeling to the image.

17

MICHAEL S. ENGEL

Cuckoo Bee—Orchid Bee, 2001

Photomacrograph made with a digital SLR camera; x4 approximate magnification

The University of Kansas, Division of Entomology, Lawrence, Kansas, United States

Made with a highly specialized imaging system that uses fiber-optic electronic flash illumination, this photograph depicts a large male of the parasitic orchid bee species, *Exaerete frontalis,* that is found in tropical South America. Like cuckoo birds, females of this "cuckoo" bee sneak into the nests of other orchid bees to lay their eggs rather than raising their own offspring. The sample is from the collection of The University of Kansas Natural History Museum.

19

Michael S. Engel

Time Flies, 2001

Photomacrograph made with a digital SLR camera; x6 approximate magnification

The University of Kansas, Division of Entomology, Lawrence, Kansas, United States

This minute fossil fly of undescribed genus and species (Diptera: Rhagionidae) is preserved as a silvery film on dark gray shale collected from a region of southern Korea. The shale dates from the Lower Cretaceous period, that is, 135–140 million years ago. Entomologists estimate the insect lived in Asia in an era just prior to the rise of flowering plants. This image was made with a highly specialized imaging system that uses fiber-optic electronic flash illumination.

José M. Estévez

I'm Always Watching You, 2000

Scanning electron photomicrograph; x150 approximate magnification;
post-capture digital colorization

Rochester Institute of Technology, Rochester, New York, United States

This fruit fly, *Drosophila melanogaster,* was preserved as a dehydrated sample from Ward's
Natural Science in Rochester, New York. Before viewing the fly in the scanning electron
microscope, the specimen was first made electrically conductive by applying a thin
layer of gold during the process known as sputter coating.

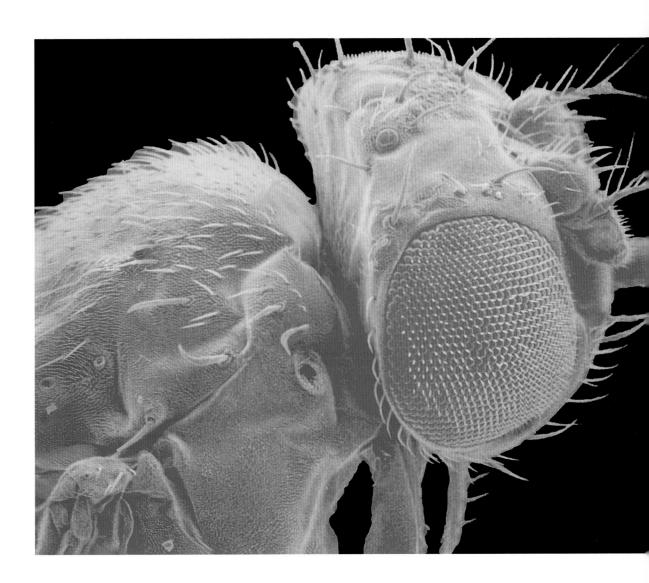

23

KARL GRIMES

Albino Axolotl, 2001

Photomacrograph; color negative film

Dublin, Ireland

An Albino Axolotl, *Ambystoma mexicanum,* or salamander, was preserved in alcohol and stored in a glass vial. The specimen's size was approximately 3 inches in length by 1 inch high. This image was originally part of the exhibition, "Future Nature," an art/science collaboration that featured unique animal embryos and fetuses that are part of the research collections of Hubrecht Laboratory, in Utrecht, The Netherlands, and the Tornblad Institute, in Lund, Sweden. The exhibition's first venue was in Dublin, Ireland, in 2002.

ADAM HARTLEY

Hg drop, ca. 1995

High-speed photograph; color negative film

The Albert Einstein College of Medicine of Yeshiva University, Bronx, New York, United States

Dr. Harold Edgerton's famous stop-motion photographs of water and milk drops served as the inspiration for this photograph. Mercury was used as the splashing material here—its shiny crown is contrasted against the oxidized surface of the mercury pool.

ADAM HARTLEY

Inedible Egg, ca. 1995

High-speed photograph; color negative film

The Albert Einstein College of Medicine of Yeshiva University, Bronx, New York, United States

This explosion of an egg was a result of the impact of a .22-caliber bullet traveling at supersonic speeds. The image was made with an E. G. & G. 541 microflash unit that provided an exposure time of 1 microsecond.

CHARLES HEDGCOCK

Male Walnut Boxing Flies, Rhagoletis boycei, *Battle for Paternal Assurance,* 1993

Photomacrograph; color transparency film; electronic flash

Arizona Research Laboratories, Division of Neurobiology, The University of Arizona, Tucson, Arizona, United States

Male boxing flies, *Rhagoletis boycei* of the family Tephritidae, fight to defend oviposition sites on an Arizona Black Walnut, *Juglans major.* Males that successfully defend these sites are permitted to mate with females prior to their ovipositing, or egg-laying, within the tree's fruit.

33

Eric J. Heller

Caustic I, 2001

Photographic simulation

Harvard University, Cambridge, Massachusetts, and Resonance Fine Art,
Lincoln, Massachusetts, United States

Rays of light from a point source have passed through two successive layers of water, each
having a wavy surface. The rays are interrupted by a plane screen located below them. The
bright patches, or "caustics," are similar to what would be observed when sunlight shines on
a swimming pool that has recently been disturbed. Recent investigations exploring the motion
of electrons in random landscapes of hills and valleys led to this curiosity in water wave
patterns. The refraction of rays at wavy surfaces is a three-dimensional analog version
of the two-dimensional electron flow that I have been studying.

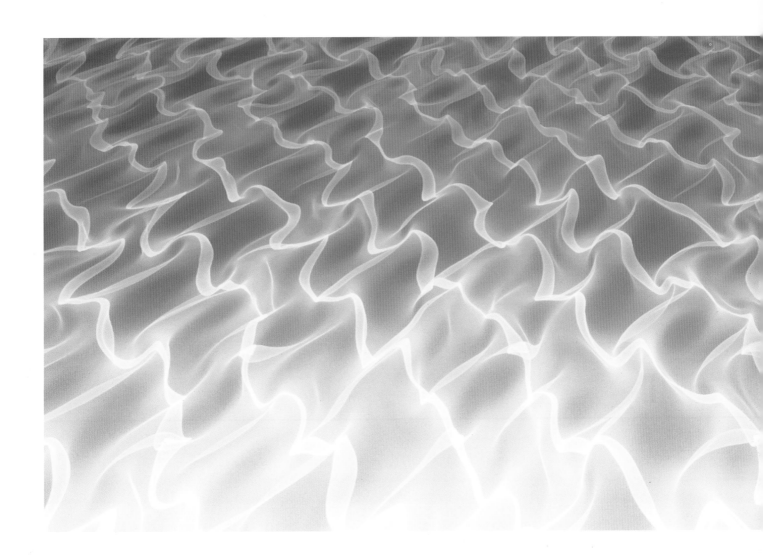

Eric J. Heller

Nanowire, 2001

Photo-realistic illustration

*Harvard University, Cambridge, Massachusetts, and Resonance Fine Art,
Lincoln, Massachusetts, United States*

Miniscule wires are becoming very important in high-tech applications. For example, they are required to pipe electrons back and forth in computer chips. Such wires, 1 micron or smaller across, are subject to imperfections in structure and performance. In these situations, the electrons traveling on the wire experience a rather bumpy ride. This situation may cause an electron to reverse its direction. This picture reveals electrons flowing to all parts of the wire from one injection point: the "sun" region. Because electrons moving in such small wires must be treated quantum mechanically, I have represented a quantum aspect of the electrons' motion with color. Electrons are really waves and in this picture, the crests of the waves are yellow while the troughs are blue. Future nanowires may have to transport electrons coherently, that is by maintaining the phase of the wave faithfully. This segment of wire is only partially successful at that process. The background shows short tracks of electrons in a bumpy land-scape similar to what is experienced inside the wire.

Hubble Heritage Team

Light and Shadow in the Carina Nebula, 2000

Astrophotograph made using the Hubble Space Telescope Wide Field Planetary Camera 2; Filters: F439W (B), F502N ([O III]), F555W (V), F656N (H-alpha), F673N ([S II]), F814W (I)

NASA and The Hubble Heritage Team of the Space Telescope Science Institute (STScI), Baltimore, Maryland, United States

Previously unseen details of a mysterious, complex structure within the Carina Nebula (NGC 3372) are revealed in this image obtained with NASA's Hubble Space Telescope. The image shows bright filaments of hot, fluorescing gas and dark silhouetted clouds of cold molecules and dust, all of which are in rapid, chaotic motion. Numerous small dark globules seen in the image may be in the process of collapsing to form new stars.

The Hubble Heritage Team is comprised of Keith Noll, Zolt Levay, Lisa Frattare, Jayanne English, Howard Bond, Carol Christian, Forrest Hamilton, and Anne Kinney—with help from astronomers Nolan Walborn, Rodolfo Barbá, and Adeline Caulet.

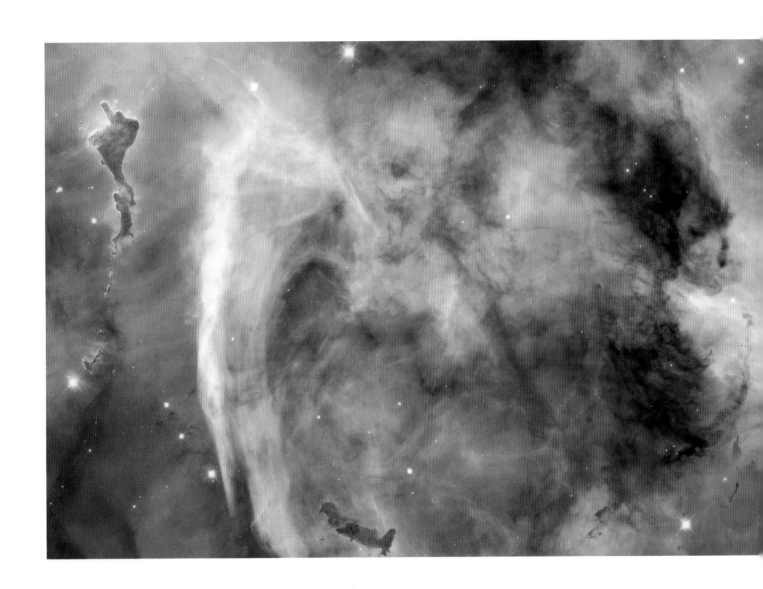

Hubble Heritage Team

The Heart of the Whirlpool Galaxy, 2001

Composite astrophotograph made with a Wide Field Planetary Camera 2 on a 0.9-meter telescope at the National Science Foundation's Kitt Peak National Observatory (NOAO/AURA) in Tucson, Arizona and the Hubble Telescope with filters: F439W (B), F547M (Stromgren y), F555W (V), F656N (Ha), F814W (I)

NASA and The Hubble Heritage Team of the Space Telescope Science Institute (STScI), Baltimore, Maryland, United States

The Whirlpool galaxy (M51) is a giant city of stars much like our own Milky Way galaxy. This composite image, in which the majority of what is seen was photographed with NASA's Hubble Space Telescope, shows the intricate spiral structure that is apparent in many large galaxies. The corners of the image were digitally composited by the Hubble Heritage Team (STScI) with archival and ground-based data collected by a team led by astronomer Keith Noll.

41

ALLEN HWANG

The Great Andromeda Galaxy, 1999

Astrophotograph made with a 6-inch Astro-Physics refractor telescope

Riverside Astronomical Society, Riverside, California, United States

Messier object 31 (M31) is known as "The Great Andromeda Galaxy." It is a beautiful spiral galaxy that is also the largest member of the Local Group of galaxies, which includes the Milky Way as well as some two dozen other smaller galaxies. It is visible on dark autumn nights as a faint, hazy patch of light that is wider than the full moon. At a distance of 2.5 million light years from earth, M31 is one of the farthest objects visible to the unaided eye.

BRUCE KAHN

Protein-DNA Complex, 2002

Image structure obtained by single crystal X-Ray diffraction; digital processing

Rochester Institute of Technology, Imaging and Photographic Technology Department, Rochester, New York, United States

This is a 3-D lenticular image of a specific DNA complex of the 65-residue, N-terminal fragment of the yeast transcriptional activator, GAL4. The image is made up of ten interlaced equiangular views of the complex structure covering 100 degrees. Individual images were rendered from the crystallographic data using ViewerLite software from Accelrys. The sequence of images was processed into the final interlaced composite using Vista Flip! software from Durst Dice America, LLC.

VIEWING INSTRUCTIONS: cover the printed image with the provided plastic lenticular screen. Align the screen with the image so that one image border is a continuous tone—either all black or all white.

44

45

BRUCE KAHN

Dust Mite, 2001

Scanning electron photomicrograph

Rochester Institute of Technology, Imaging and Photographic Technology Department, Rochester, New York, United States

This image of a dust mite, *Dermatophagoides farinae,* was photographed with an ISI Super IIIA SEM. The mite was attached to the sample stub using conductive tape, and was not coated. The accelerating voltage was 2 kV, and the magnification x700.

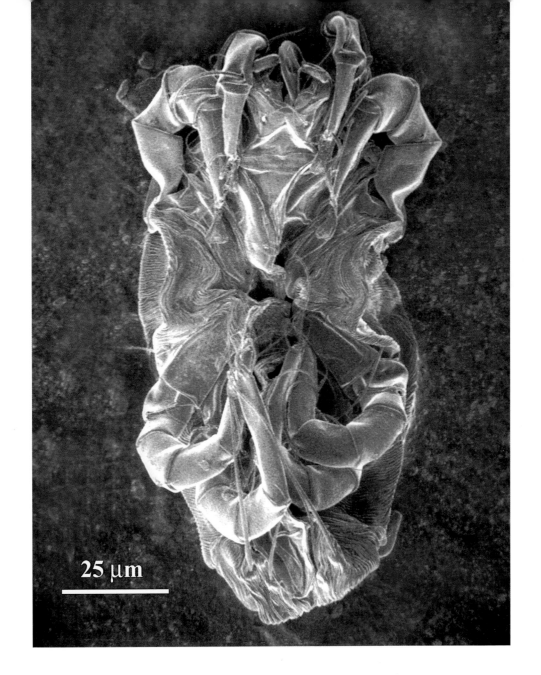

25 μm

47

Roy Kaltschmidt

Microbes in Basalt, 2000

Digital photomicrograph; illuminated with infrared energy and electronic flash;
post-capture digital composite

Lawrence Berkeley National Laboratory, Berkeley, California, United States

Columbia River basalts from beneath the Idaho National Engineering and Environmental
Laboratory were found to harbor 85 strains of soil-dwelling microorganisms. Researchers
studied living colonies of the microbes in thin slices from unaltered basalt cores by using an
infrared beamline at the Advanced Light Source of Lawrence Berkeley National Laboratory.
This technique has produced spectacular success in establishing the role of microbes in
detoxifying carcinogenic and radioactive pollutant waste areas.

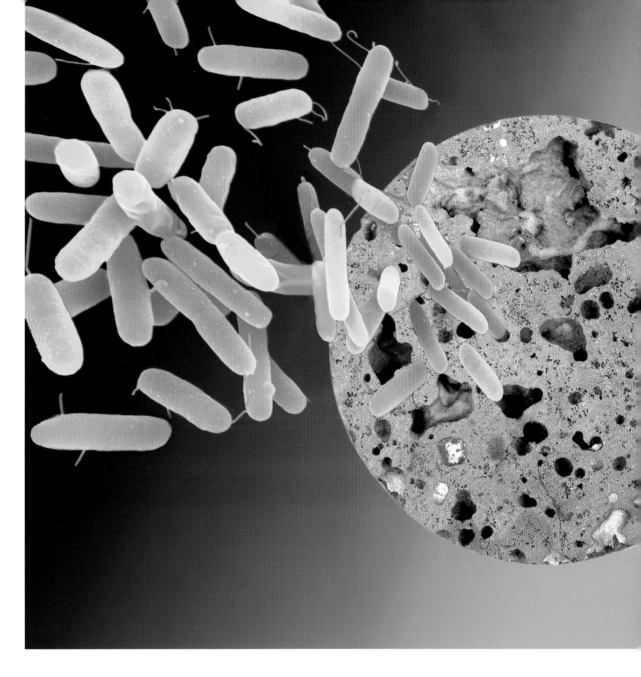

EDWARD KINSMAN

Rotation Streak Digital Camera Stability Test, 2001

Digital composite photograph

Kinsman Physics Productions, Rochester, New York

Nine hundred individual images of a bouquet of roses on a rotation table make up this composite photograph. This imaging technique measures the stability of various digital camera systems. In this instance, the majority of the individual images are uniform and the camera passes the stability test. Each separate image is apparent upon close inspection of the composite picture.

Harald Kleine

Shock Wave Diffraction around a Cylinder, 1993

Reconstructed holographic interferogram

Stosswellenlabor RWTH, Aachen, Germany, and Tohoku University, Sendai, Japan

The original hologram was obtained through use of a ruby laser at 694 nm, pulse energy 1 J, pulse width 30 ns, and was captured on a holographic plate (10 cm x 15 cm). The hologram was reconstructed with a He-Ne laser (λ= 632.8 nm, 10 mW, cw) onto medium-format monochromatic film.

The photograph shows a shock wave traveling in a vertical direction, from bottom to top, with a speed of 770 m/s and diffracting around a cylinder. Apart from the primary diffracted and reflected shocks, this process generated a number of shear layers, vortices, and secondary shock waves. The cylinder had a diameter of 2 cm; the flow was generated in a shock tube with a square cross-section of 5.4 cm x 5.4 cm. The observed phenomenon is a shock wave in nitrogen (N_2) of subatmospheric initial pressure (p_i = 25 kPa).

The picture was taken under the supervision of Professor Hans Grönig, RWTH, Aachen.

EUGENE KOWALUK

Omega Target Shot, 1987

Small-format color transparency made with multiple teleconverters and a telephoto lens

University of Rochester, Laboratory for Laser Energetics, Rochester, New York, United States

Twenty-four high-power laser beams are focused on a one-millimeter gold-coated ball that creates a very high-temperature ionized gas visible in this photograph as bright spots. The laser beams each have a peak power approximately equal to the instantaneous electric power production of the United States. The pressure conditions on the target amount to tens of millions of atmospheres. These experiments are being carried out to develop inertial fusion as an energy source.

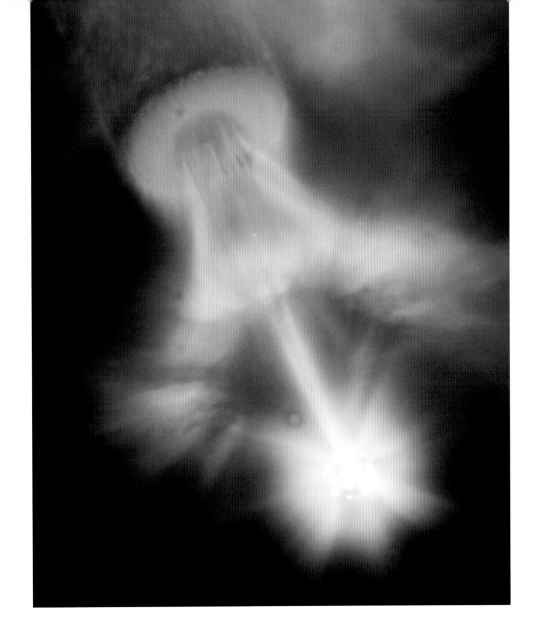

KEVIN LANGTON

Human Iris, 2000

Slitlamp biomicrograph; x2 approximate magnification

Columbia University, Department of Ophthalmology, New York, New York, United States

This photograph was recorded with the AVI digital slitlamp biomicroscope. It demonstrates a normal pigment distribution pattern found in the iris of a healthy adult.

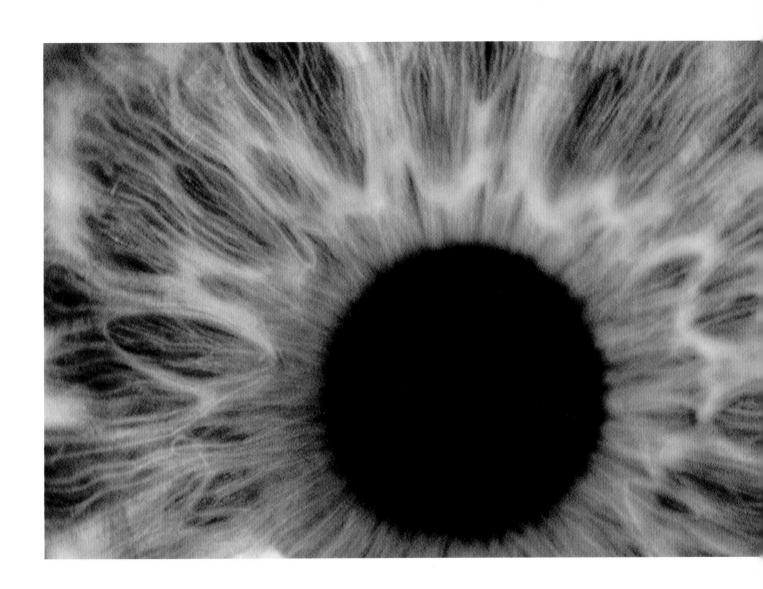

57

Roy Larimer

Organic Lace, 2001

Photomacrograph made with a digital SLR camera system

Microptics, Inc., Yonkers, New York, United States

The features of this tiny Peruvian lace bug of the family Tingidae, are recorded in exquisite color, detail, and fine texture. Capturing the lace bug in a single shot required finely controlled lighting in order to achieve both depth and resolution. The 8-mm long insect was photographed with reflected and transmitted electronic flash light delivered by a fiber-optic system. The specimen was photographed through the courtesy of the American Museum of Natural History, New York.

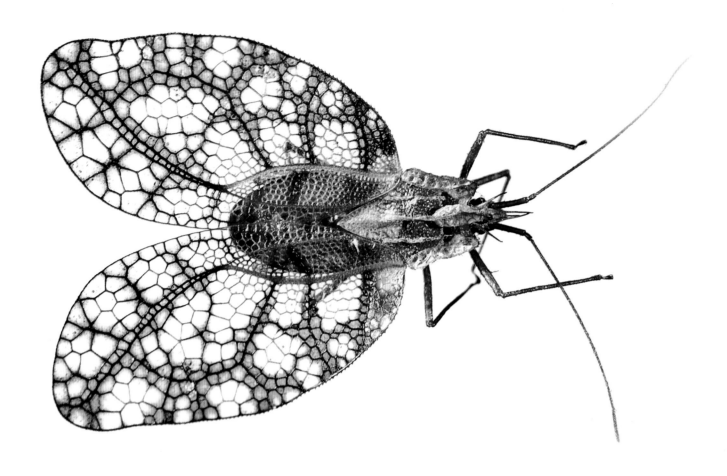

59

Roy Larimer

Clearly a Fish, 2001

Photomacrograph made with a digital SLR camera system

Microptics, Inc., Yonkers, New York, United States

This Cichlid fish, *Paratilapia* sp. (Cichlidae), measured 4 cm from nose to tail. The specimen was clarified and stained before submersion in a clear vessel filled with alcohol. It was then illuminated from three directions. Additional transmitted light eliminated shadows in the photographic setup. The specimen was photographed through the courtesy of the American Museum of Natural History, New York.

61

Philip LaRock

Digital Moon, 2001

Digital composite astrophotograph

Copyright Eastman Kodak Company, Rochester, New York, United States

Multiple monochromatic images were captured with a Kodak DCS 660M camera through Rochester Institute of Technology's 16-inch Cassegrain telescope, prime focused. Fourteen images were assembled, registered, balanced and blended using Adobe Photoshop.

DAVID MALIN

A Cometary Globule, CG-4, 1991

Composite astrophotograph

Copyright Anglo-Australian Observatory. Photograph by David Malin, Sydney, Australia.

Dusty clouds in the Milky Way galaxy are normally hidden except when they obscure background stars. However, the dark dust of CG-4 is feebly illuminated by light from a nearby star cluster. This light also blows away some of the dusty material in the object's comet-like tail. The red color arises from hydrogen fluorescing in the ultraviolet component of the incident starlight. CG-4's cloud contains enough gas to make close to 60 Sun-like stars. The photograph covers a field of about 22-arc minutes across, or 10 light years at the distance of CG-4.

The original image was captured with the Anglo-Australian telescope (equivalent to a 12.7 m focal length, f/3.3 reflecting objective), on three hypersensitized, monochrome photographic plates with filters that recorded the red, blue, and green bands separately. Each of the three images was photographically amplified to enhance faint detail. The images were then recombined on color negative film to produce a true-color image.

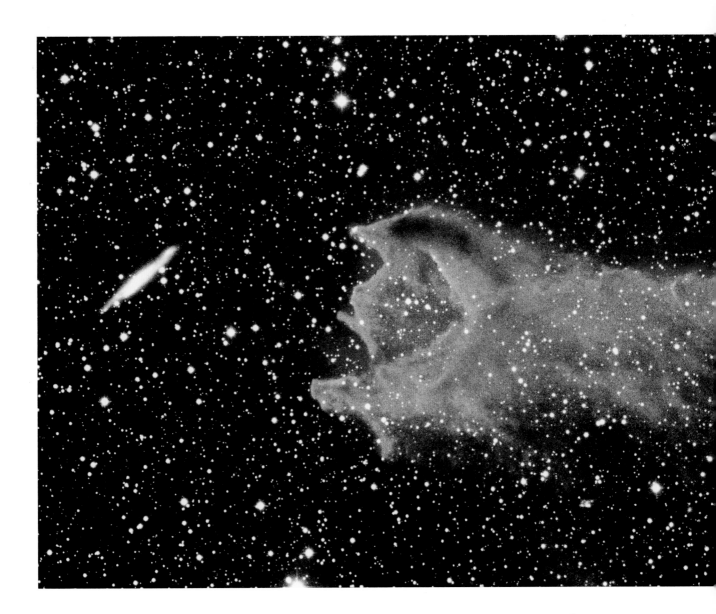

David Malin

The Great Nebula in Orion, 1988

Composite astrophotograph

Copyright Anglo-Australian Observatory/Royal Observatory, Edinburgh.
Photograph from UK Schmidt plates by David Malin, Sydney, Australia.

The Orion nebula is the nearest major star-forming region at a distance of roughly 1,500 light years. It is composed of dust, gas, and bright stars—many of which are recent formations within the nebula. The picture is about 58-arc minutes wide, corresponding to approximately 25 light years at the distance of the nebula.

The UK Schmidt Telescope (equivalent to a 3.05 m focal length, f/2.5 reflecting objective), was used to sequentially expose three hypersensitized monochrome photographic plates with separate filters that recorded red, green, and blue light. Each monochrome image was subject to photographic unsharp-masking to extract detail in high densities. The images were then recombined on color negative film to produce a true-color image.

KATHLEEN McCARTHY AND MATTHEW H. SMITH

Polarized Landscape #4, New York, 2002

Digital composite photograph

New York, New York, and Madison, Alabama, United States

While color and brightness are familiar concepts to most, the polarization state of light is largely unfamiliar to humans since human eyes are almost completely insensitive to this spectrum. The state of polarization is represented as color in this image, revealing the striking pattern present in a clear blue sky. Some animal species, such as bees, use this polarization pattern as a navigational aid. The image was created from several digital images that were captured with polarizers. The images were then subject to mathematical post-analysis and synthesis.

69

JOHN MCLANE

Sea Salt, 1996

Scanning electron photomicrograph

Rocky River, Ohio, United States

This salt crystal was derived from a Pacific Ocean water sample from the Oregon coast. The crystal was grown on a glass slide by adding methanol to the seawater, which accelerates the evaporation process and produces a salt hopper. The photograph was made using a JEOL 840 scanning electron microscope.

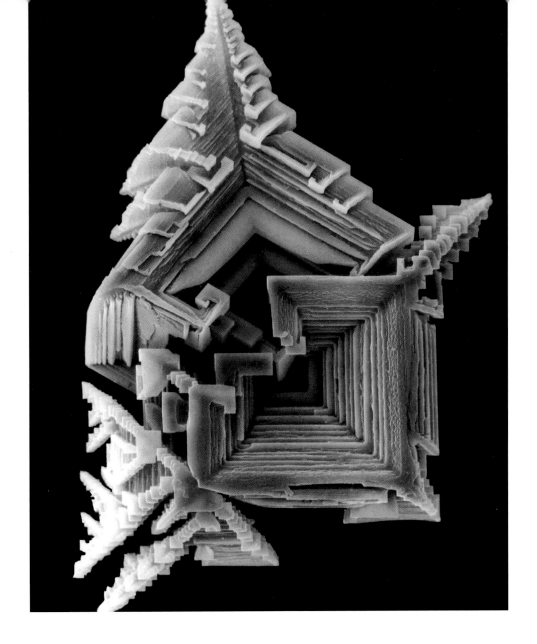

Oliver Meckes and Nicole Ottawa

Lavender Leaf, 1999

Scanning electron photomicrograph; x590 approximate magnification;
post-capture digital colorization

Eye of Science, Reutlingen, Germany

The image shows a small portion of a leaf from a lavender plant, *Lavandula angustifolia.*
Numerous dense branched hairs, called trichromes, are observed in the picture covering
the leaf's surface. These hairs function as a protective barrier against the invasion of pests
and also serve to reduce water evaporation from the leaf. The rounded structure (pale tan,
lower center) is an oil gland that produces lavender's aromatic scent. Below the gland is
the impermeable cuticle that is supported by epidermal cells. The color in this image
was digitally added afterwards since scanning electron microscopes are only capable
of producing monochrome images.

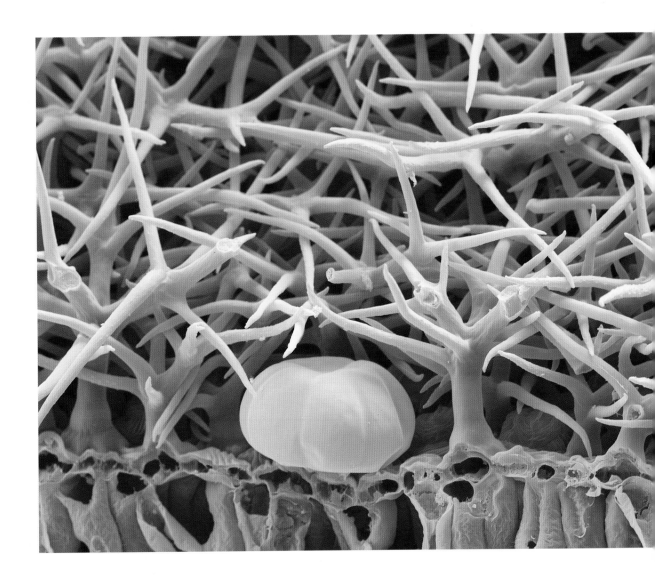

73

Oliver Meckes and Nicole Ottawa

Macrophage and Borrelia burgdorferi, 2000

Scanning electron photomicrograph; x1,000 approximate magnification;
post-capture digital colorization

Eye of Science, Reutlingen, Germany

A macrophage, or white blood cell (shown in yellow), is observed attacking a group of *Borrelia* sp. bacteria (colored blue, lower left). Various types of *Borrelia* sp. bacteria cause conditions such as Lyme disease and relapsing fever. The macrophage here has extended a long pseudopod towards the bacteria prior to engulfing them. Once engulfed the bacteria will be destroyed through a process known as phagocytosis, a type of chemical digestion. Macrophages combat many types of foreign organisms that infiltrate the body, including bacteria.

GARY S. MICHALEC

Tubaria furfuracea, *Fringed Tubaria Mushroom Gills*, 1999

Close-up photograph; color transparency film; electronic flash

*Veterans Administration Medical Center, Ophthalmic Imaging,
Minneapolis, Minnesota, United States*

Photographs for nature and science applications are both challenging and interesting to make. The photograph of this gill pattern on the bottom of a mushroom cap was difficult to achieve because of the perspective needed to reveal structure while preserving a pleasing aesthetic composition.

Claudia R. Murphy

Coyote Palate Bone, 1989

Photomacrograph; color transparency film

White Plains, New York, United States

Photomacrography and photomicrography are complex because they require precise control of many technical issues, including a limited range of focus. As a consequence, special approaches are sometimes necessary. In this photograph, I attempted to reveal the bony structure of a coyote hard palate through the use of "Nilssonian lighting." This lighting method, named for Lennart Nilsson, employs optical staining of specific structures, along with strong colorization to emphasize the structures' visual presence.

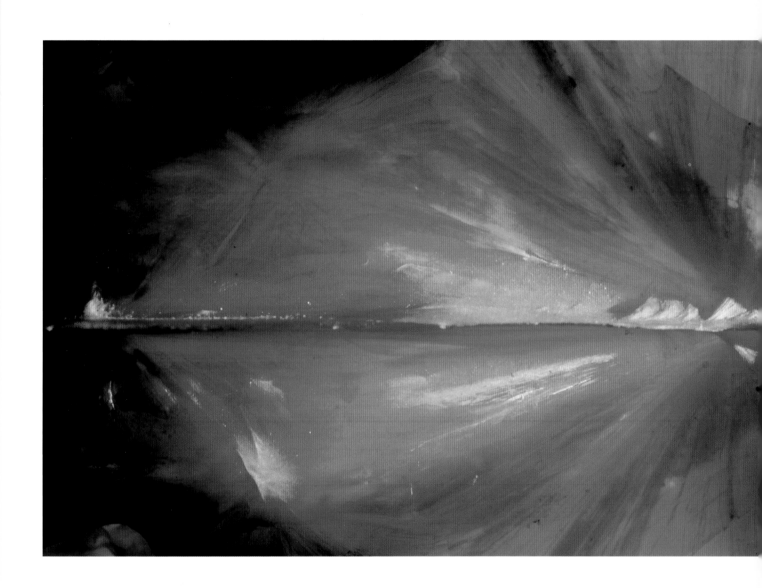

TAM C. NGUYEN

Hirtodrosophila *n. sp. from Vietnam,* 2001

Photomicrograph made with brightfield illumination

American Museum of Natural History, Division of Invertebrate Zoology,
New York, New York, United States

This new species of fly was collected from the Vietnam Central Highlands in 1999. The genitalia of different flies have subtle variations that can be used to distinguish different species. The genital organs shown here in this female specimen are typical of *Hirtodrosophila.* The most prominent feature is the oviscapt with the highly sclerotized pegs or teeth.

83

Joe Ogrodnick

Mosquito: Emerging Adult, 1983

Color photomacrographs made with electronic flash; post-capture digital composite

Cornell University, New York State Agricultural Experiment Station,
Geneva, New York, United States

In its pupal stage mosquitoes have a comma-shaped form which, unless disturbed, floats at the surface of the water while breathing through two small tubes called trumpets. When it is time for the adult to emerge from the pupal case, the insect straightens its abdomen—a cue to prepare to start photographing. The insect then uses pressure from trapped air beneath the pupal skin to split the case and emerge as an adult mosquito. In the first frame of this series the fissure can be seen on top of the pupal case. The transformation occurred in a petri dish that held mosquito larvae, water, and aquatic plants.

84

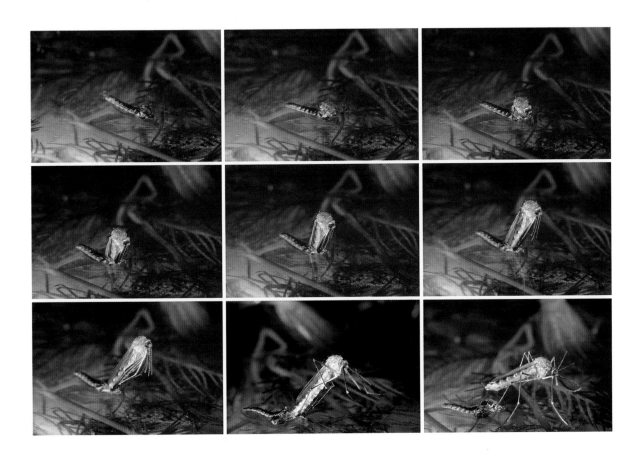

ANNI PAYNE

Pregnant Flea, 2000

Photomicrograph; x100 approximate magnification

Milk and Honey Photography, Clovelly, Australia

The common water flea, of the family Daphniidae, is found in most bodies of water. It is a valuable food source for animals such as fish and newts. The water flea's transparent body offers a clear view of all their body systems—making them ideal subjects for examination with a microscope. The water flea pictured here has just eaten a meal of green algae that appears as a green line through its digestive tract. The other circular forms in its body are developing eggs. The immature flea at left has also recently eaten.

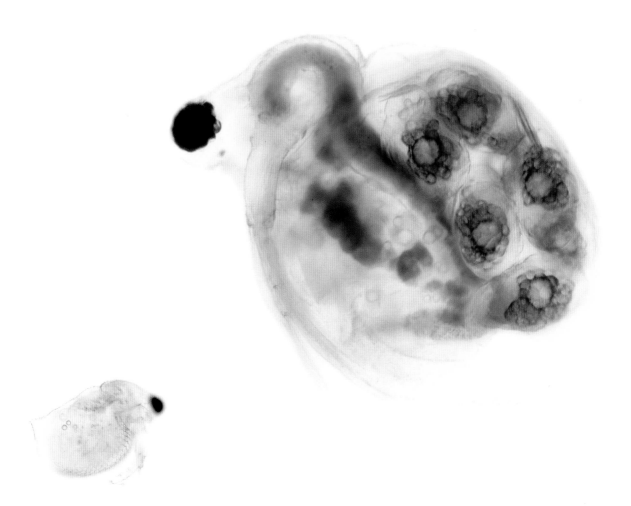

87

Kevin A. Raskoff

Cliopsis krohni, 2001

Close-up photograph; color transparency film; electronic flash

Monterey Bay Aquarium Research Institute, Moss Landing, California, United States

Cliopsis krohni is a pelagic snail of the order Gymnosomata, which thrives in the open waters of the Atlantic Ocean. This specimen was approximately 7 cm long.

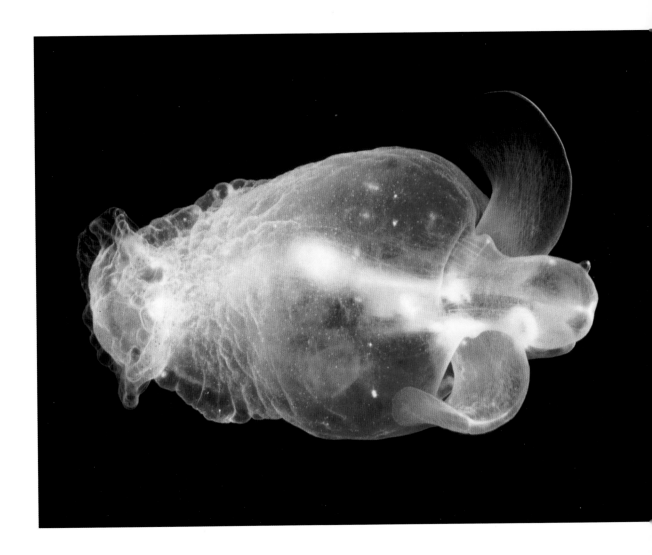

KEVIN A. RASKOFF

Orchistoma pileus, 2001

Close-up photograph; color transparency film; electronic flash

Monterey Bay Aquarium Research Institute, Moss Landing, California, United States

The photograph of this hydromedusa of the order Leptomedusae, was taken while blue-water diving far off the coast of Massachusetts. The expedition was part of a research project that catalogued gelatinous animals found in open ocean. The specimen measured approximately 5 cm in diameter.

Amanda Rebbechi

Epilepsy Procedure, 2000

Close-up photograph; color transparency film; electronic flash

Prince of Wales Hospital, Medical Illustration Unit, Randwick, Australia

This photograph documents the surgical procedure of placing intracranial electrodes on the surface of an epilepsy patient's brain. The electrode grid shown here records brain functions and aids in localizing the source of the patient's seizures. Surgical photography poses various challenges because of concerns for a sterile field and the exposure to infection. In neurosurgery the risk of infection is significantly heightened and the making of surgical photographs often requires additional precautions.

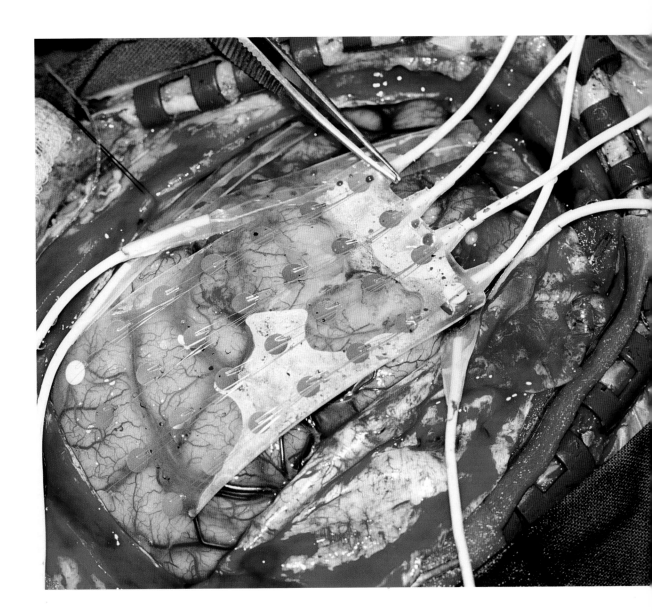

93

Amanda Rebbechi

Adult Human Brain, 2000

Specimen photograph; transparency film; studio electronic flash

Prince of Wales Hospital, Medical Illustration Unit, Randwick, Australia

This photograph was made for illustrative purposes on location in the hospital mortuary.

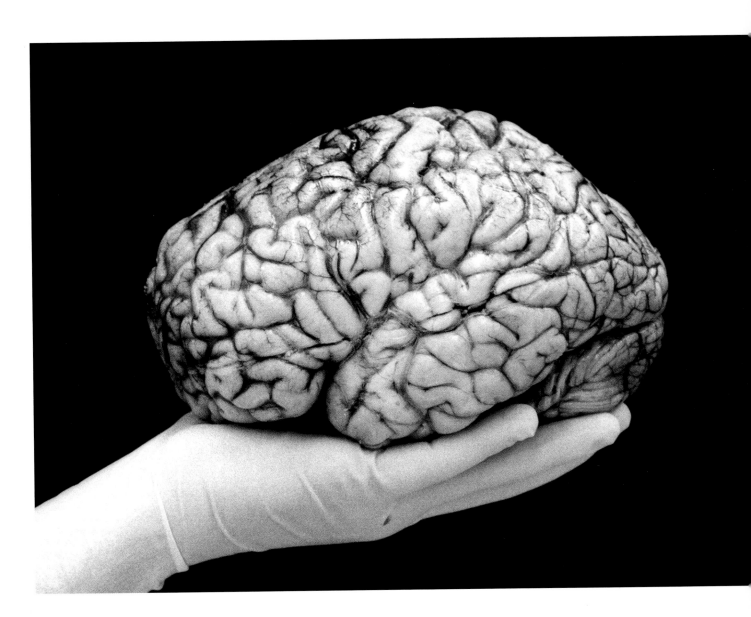

95

David C. Ring

Bar-coded Honeybee on Honeycomb, 1988

Photomacrograph

Arizona Health Sciences Center, Division of Biomedical Communications,
The University of Arizona, Tucson, Arizona, United States

A miniaturized bar code affixed to the back of this honeybee was scanned with a laser bar code reader in order to track how frequently the bee left and returned to the hive. Additional information was also gathered relative to the duration of these trips. This photograph required a long exposure of approximately 10 seconds at f/22, during which a tungsten-balanced macro light was used to briefly illuminate the honeybee and comb. The bee's environment was pre-cooled to allow positioning of the bee in the photographic setup. Care was taken to allow the environment to warm up prior to the moment of flight, thus preserving the bee's natural appearance.

Nile Root

Monte Balmaceda Glacier, Patagonia, Chile, 2001

Landscape photograph; color negative film; post-capture digitization

Tucson, Arizona, United States

Monte Balmaceda is viewed here from the Ultima Esperanza Fiord. The mountain is just 2,035 meters high but it is in an almost perpetual state of storm. Consequently only a few documented ascents are known. The glacier seen off the eastern slopes of Monte Balmaceda is receding in a manner similar to many of the planet's other glaciers. Scientists suggest that glacial recession is a result of global warming. The photographer is a Professor Emeritus at Rochester Institute of Technology.

KRISTIN ROYALTY

Butterfly Wing, 2002

Photomicrograph made with darkfield illumination; x25 magnification

Rochester Institute of Technology, Biomedical Photographic Communications,
Rochester, New York, United States

The small brown structure in the center of this picture is an artifact that was accidentally included in this prepared butterfly wing slide specimen. I found it to be an interesting focal point for the photograph as it contrasted with the wing's iridescent scales. After trying several different lighting techniques, darkfield illumination provided the most dramatic effect. The image was made during a photomicrography course in RIT's department of Biomedical Photographic Communications.

SETH RUFFINS

15dpc Embryonic Mouse, 2001

Composite photograph from magnetic resonance imaging (MRI) system images

California Institute of Technology, Beckman Institute, Pasadena, California, United States

The development of a 15-day post-conception (dpc) mouse embryo is charted here. This visualization is part of the Caltech "μMRI Atlas of Mouse Development" project. The image data was collected using MRI, which is a non-optical imaging technique that uses the magnetic properties of protons in a chemical environment to generate image contrast. The first two images are volumetric renderings of MRI data with different transparency settings. Note that the center image permits the visualization of internal structures. The image at right shows the surface rendering of segmented anatomy. Segmentation allows each anatomical structure to be visualized, "handled," and explored as an independent object within the context of the entire embryo.

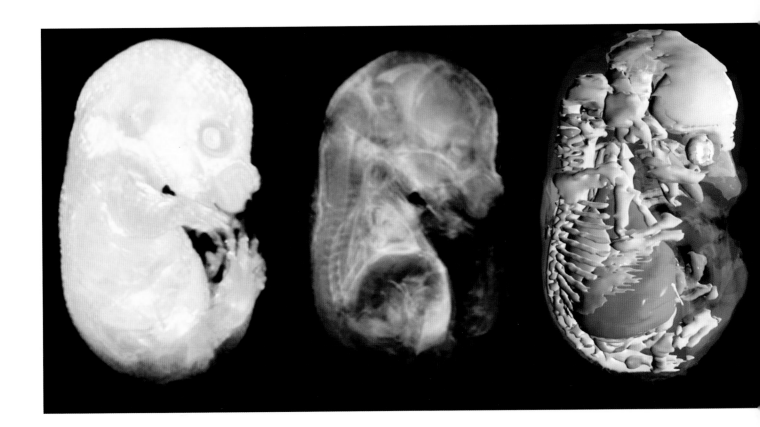

Patrick J. Saine

Retina Blues, 1999

Digital composite photograph made from a series of digital fundus (retinal) images

Dartmouth-Hitchcock Medical Center, Lebanon, New Hampshire, United States

This composite image was created by using Photoshop to manipulate and colorize mono-chrome frames from a fluorescein angiogram taken with a fundus camera. Photographs of the patient's fundus, or retina, were taken; then the sodium fluorescein dye was injected into the patient's arm vein. The dye was photographed as it filled the choroidal and retinal blood vessels. A matched pair of exciter and barrier filters maximized the dye's fluorescence.

Ophthalmic photography provides an ideal fabric from which to construct digital quilts of interesting shapes and patterns. The retinal images that make up this photograph are hidden from a normal world-view—an ironic twist since the eye itself is the organ of sight.

Kristen G. Toohey

Common Marmoset, Callithrix jacchus, 2000

Composite color transparency made with a macro camera system and light microscope

Harvard Medical School, New England Regional Primate Research Center, Southborough, Massachusetts, United States

This image series shows a magnification progression of the Common Marmoset monkey from the whole body down through detail perceptible at the cellular level. The original intention was to photograph the whole fetal image; however, when magnified for closer inspection, the intriguing picture in the foot was observed. At a magnification of x12.5, the bizarre likeness of the face in one of the toes was discovered. The three images were combined to record this scientific oddity.

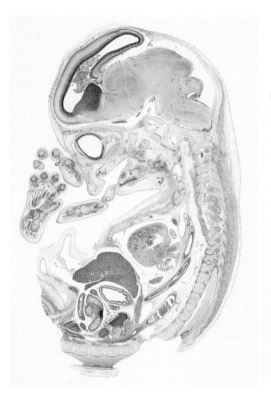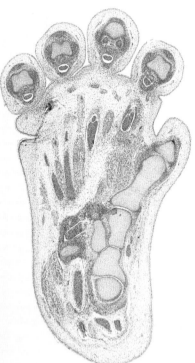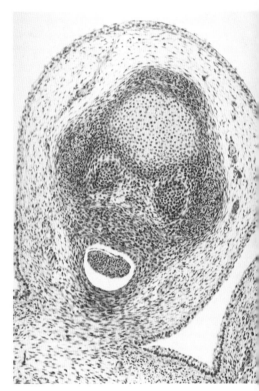

Susanne K. Williams and Adrian Dyer

Seeing Through Straws, 2001

Photographic simulation of insect vision

Royal Melbourne Institute of Technology, Applied Science Photography, Melbourne, Australia

Photography was used in this experiment as a tool to provide a simulation of insect vision. A bundle of 4,500 black drinking straws were tied together to selectively allow light from the subject to fall onto a 14- by 14-inch ground glass screen. The resolution of the system was created to be equivalent to that of a fly's eye. The resulting image formed on the ground glass was then captured with a medium-format camera. The sitter in the portrait is Professor W. R. Muntz, a Monash University biologist, who has studied cephalopod vision, specifically in *Nautilus* spp.

Loren M. Winters

Deceleration of a Projectile by an Elastic Strip, 1992

High-speed sequential photograph

The North Carolina School of Science and Mathematics, Durham, North Carolina, United States

A hanging elastic strip caught a 4.5-mm spherical projectile that moved from left to right. The projectile and strip are seen in this photograph at eight successive instants of time, which begin immediately after the projectile contacts the first strip. Eight flash units were covered with different colored filters to provide visual separation of the overlapping images. The time interval between flashes was 0.00055 seconds. The strip decelerates the projectile from 130 to 7 m/s in approximately 0.004 seconds. The decelerating force is applied primarily by the stretching of the elastic immediately behind the projectile.

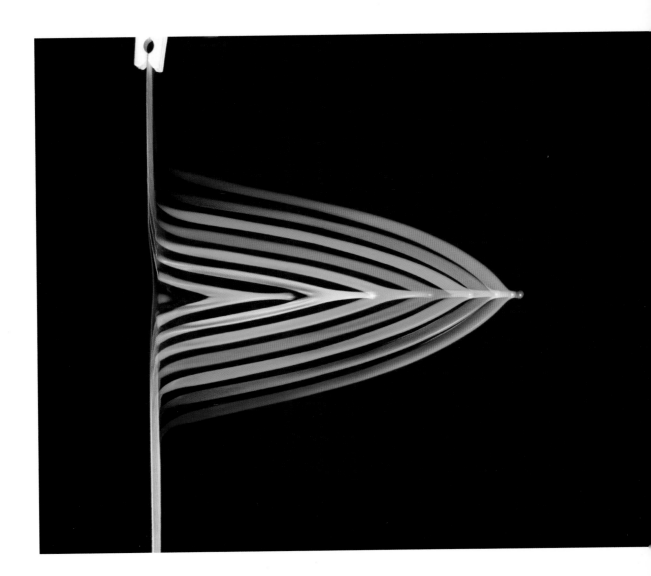

ALSON WONG

Total Solar Eclipse, Chisamba, Zambia, 2001

Composite astrophotograph made with a Vixen 102-ED refracting telescope

Riverside Astronomical Society, Riverside, California, United States

A total solar eclipse occurs when the moon's disk covers the disk of the sun. The total solar eclipse of June 21, 2001, was the first of the twenty-first century. Visible from the Southern Hemisphere, the path of totality crossed the South Atlantic Ocean, southern Africa, and Madagascar. The Sun's outer atmosphere, the corona, can only be seen from Earth during a total solar eclipse. Because of the tremendous range in brightness between the inner and outer corona, it is impossible to capture all of its detail in a single photograph. Eleven separate exposures ranging from 1/1000th to one second were scanned and then digitally combined to create a single image which shows the range of detail normally visible when viewing the corona directly. Around the edge of the moon's dark shadow, pink prominences can be seen as they erupt from the sun's surface.

KENT WOOD

Comet Hyakutake, Polaris, Big Dipper and Saguaro, 1996

Astrophotograph made using a time exposure of 12 min. at f/2.8; color transparency film

Albuquerque, New Mexico, United States

This photograph was made on March 27, 1996, in the Arizona Desert near Florence, Arizona. While the stars exhibit trails due to the rotation of the earth during the exposure, the Comet's head is relatively sharp because it was in close proximity to Polaris.

KENT WOOD

Lightning Strike with a Second Upward Streamer, 1987

Landscape photograph made using a time exposure of unknown duration at f/5.6; color transparency film

Albuquerque, New Mexico, United States

This strike was photographed on a hot August night during a thunderstorm in the foothills of the Santa Catalina Mountains that border Tucson to the north. This photograph shows two positive upward streamers, one that created a bolt on the left and a second upward streamer on the right that is unconnected.

BARBARA BAKER BURROWS

Barbara Baker Burrows began her career with *LIFE* magazine 35 years ago as a picture researcher and was promoted to picture editor in 1987. Her major responsibilities included the coordination of the magazine's photographic coverage at major events, as well as overseeing the production of *LIFE*'s special issues and book projects. She has also curated numerous retrospective exhibitions, such as those featuring the photography of Alfred Eisenstaedt, George Silk, and Larry Burrows. Her recent editorial work includes the book, *One Nation; America Remembers September 11, 2001.*

IAN GATLEY

Dr. Ian Gatley is the Dean of the College of Science and Director of the Chester F. Carlson Center for Imaging Science at Rochester Institute of Technology. Dr. Gatley previously directed the Infrared Astronomy program at the National Optical Astronomy Observatory in Tucson, Arizona. There he headed the committee that developed area-array-based cameras and spectrometers, which have improved science productivity by a factor of millions. Further details about Dr. Gatley's career can be found at *http://www.cis.rit.edu/people/faculty/gatley/.*

RICK HOCK

Rick Hock is Director of Exhibitions and Program Design at George Eastman House, International Museum of Photography and Film in Rochester, New York. He has organized several major exhibitions such as "Seeing the Unseen: Dr. Harold E. Edgerton and the Wonders of Strobe Alley" and "The Pencil of Nature: Photography's Trace and Transformation." He is the recipient of two National Endowment for the Arts fellowships and his photographic work is held in several major collections including The Museum of Modern Art, New York, and the Philadelphia Museum of Art.

STAFFAN LARSSON

Staffan Larsson is the Director of Medical Media at the Huddinge University Hospital in Stockholm, Sweden. Mr. Larsson has been active in scientific and medical photography since 1973. He serves as director of international contacts and education for the Swedish Society of Medical and Technical Photographers (FMTF). Mr. Larsson also helped establish and now acts as Board secretary for the Lennart Nilsson Award—a prize for innovative scientific photography named in honor of the renowned Swedish photographer.

WILLIE OSTERMAN

Willie Osterman joined RIT in 1984 and is a professor in the School of Photographic Arts and Sciences, where he is also Chair of the Master of Fine Art Photography. He has lectured and taught workshops around the world on the subjects of creativity, the Zone System, museum practices, and fine art printing. Professor Osterman was the recipient of the RIT Gitner Prize in 2001 for his book entitled *Déjà View: Bologna, Italy*—recently released in its second edition.

RICHARD RABINOWITZ

Richard Rabinowitz is the Vice President and Group Publisher of *American Photo* and *Popular Photography* magazines, a position he has held since 1991. He has also been executive producer of 32 television specials that center on photography, including the Emmy Award-winning, "Freeze Frame Switzerland" which aired on The Travel Channel.

SUSAN A. SMITH

Susan Smith is the Assistant Director of Photography at *National Geographic Magazine* in Washington, D.C. She has worked for the publication a total of 31 years, and has served in her current capacity since 1990. Ms. Smith coordinates the magazine's summer photography internship program where she identifies and develops the talent of young location photographers and administrative staff.

MICHAEL PERES

Michael Peres is the Chair of Biomedical Photographic Communications in the School of Photographic Arts and Sciences at RIT and teaches courses in photomicrography, photomacrography, and bio-medical photography. He has authored numerous publications, presented over a hundred oral papers, and conducted more than 30 workshops on such topics as "Imaging through the Microscope." He has also taught workshops on producing QuickTime Virtual Reality movies that have taken him to a variety of international locations, including Sweden, Tanzania, Germany, and Australia. He has been an active member of the BioCommunications Association for 24 years and belongs to the Ophthalmic Photographers' Society. He is currently serving as the Chair of the Lennart Nilsson Award Nominating Committee as well as the Co-Coordinator of the RIT Big Shot project.

ANDREW DAVIDHAZY

Andrew Davidhazy is a professor in RIT's School of Photographic Arts and Sciences and Chair of its Imaging and Photographic Technology Department. He specializes in high-speed photography and photo-instrumentation. He has published and exhibited widely and been invited to speak or present at conferences, workshops, and seminars worldwide. He was a NASA/ASEE Research Fellow at NASA Langley Research Center in Virginia, as well as the first Kodak Visiting Professor to Australia. He also served as guest instructor at The Institute for Photography of the University of Gothenberg in Sweden. Davidhazy received the RIT Eisenhart Award for Outstanding Teaching and was granted the Professor Raymond C. Bowman Award from the Society for Imaging Science and Technology along with the Society's 2001 Fellowship award. He collaborated with Drs. Leslie Stroebel and Ronald Francis on an investigation for the House Select Committee on the assassination of President Kennedy and has consulted on scientific photography and photographic instrumentation for many industrial and governmental agencies. He is an active member of The Society for Imaging Science and Technology (IS&T) and The International Society for Optical Engineering (SPIE).

FROM THE BEGINNING, we knew *Images from Science* would require significant collaborations in order to achieve the results we envisioned. At each phase of the project's evolution, we received valuable input, suggestions, and support that allowed us to reach the next step in the process. In the context of this brief statement, we cannot begin to express the gratitude we feel to all of the various contributors who made the book and exhibition possible but we wish to formally recognize their contributions as best as we can.

Since first sharing the idea with the RIT community, we have received tremendous encouragement. Frank Cost, Richard Zakia, Paul Stella, Bill DuBois, Roberley Bell, and Patti Ambrogi all helped in brainstorming ways to make the project a reality. When the four-color catalogue became part of the vision, we received positive feedback from David Pankow, Curator of the RIT Cary Graphic Arts Collection and head of Cary Graphic Arts Press. He aided in developing a preliminary publication plan and cost estimate that resulted in the organization of a mini-fundraiser. We extend very special thanks to the following *Images from Science* partners for their generous financial support: Elizabeth Garcia from Carl Zeiss, Inc; James Jarmusch from Topcon America Corporation; Jeff Karp, head of Rollei USA, LLC; Henry Schleichkorn and Mike Fisher, owners of Custom Medical Stock Photo, Inc.; Laurel Price Jones and Deborah McKinzie from the RIT Office of Development; Dr. Ian Gatley, Dean, RIT College of Science; the Faculty Evaluation and Development (FEAD) Grant committee from the RIT College of Imaging Arts and Sciences; Art Shufelt and Bill Conger from Durst Dice America, LLC; and Dr. Hans Wigzell and the Board of the Lennart Nilsson Award Foundation in Stockholm, Sweden.

A preliminary outline was all we had to propose to David Malin, photographic scientist from the Anglo-Australian Observatory in Sydney, Australia—yet he volunteered at once to write the guest essay for the book. His insightful words provide a strong introduction to the images selected for the exhibition. Dr. Joan Stone, Dean of the RIT College of Imaging Arts and Sciences, also extended her support by contributing a thoughtful foreword. Lennart Nilsson, one of the giants of modern scientific photography, generously endorsed *Images from Science* and submitted one of his most stunning images for publication. We are grateful to many others who simply promoted our idea, including Donna Sterlace, Roy Larimer, Kevin Langton, and a host of web sites and journals that shared the opportunity with their readers.

Once the photographs were submitted, a prestigious group of seven judges did a wonderful job of selecting the work that comprises the exhibition. We first invited Susan Smith from *National Geographic Magazine*. Susan's immediate support was a huge esteem-builder that gave us the confidence to approach the remaining judges for our panel. They were: Mr. Richard Rabinowitz from *American Photo* magazine; Dr. Ian Gatley from the RIT Carlson Center for Imaging Science; Mr. Staffan Larsson from Huddinge Hospital in Sweden; Professor Willie Osterman, from the RIT School of Photographic Arts and Sciences; Ms. Barbara Baker Burrows from *LIFE* magazine; and Mr. Rick Hock from George Eastman House, International Museum of Photography and Film.

In closing, we wish to note that the production of this catalogue with its myriad imagery and technical complexities represents a formidable accomplishment. We wish to especially acknowledge the heroic efforts of Amelia Hugill-Fontanel, Production Editor, Cary Graphic Arts Press. She managed every detail of the production process with amazing skill and met every challenge posed by an accelerated schedule. Melissa Kaup-Augustine of Lizard Press handled the book design beautifully. Erich Lehman of RIT's School of Print Media was helpful in proofing the catalogue's reproductions. Finally, we thank our copy editor, John Sippel, and Laura Jaffe, Raymond Chan, and Julian Lui from InterPress Ltd.

M. P. and A. D.

CARL ZEISS, INC.

CUSTOM MEDICAL STOCK PHOTO/helpMD.com, INC.

DURST DICE AMERICA, LLC

LENNART NILSSON AWARD FOUNDATION

RIT CARY GRAPHIC ARTS PRESS

RIT CHESTER F. CARLSON CENTER FOR IMAGING SCIENCE

RIT COLLEGE OF IMAGING ARTS AND SCIENCES

RIT OFFICE OF DEVELOPMENT

RIT SCHOOL OF PHOTOGRAPHIC ARTS AND SCIENCES

ROLLEI, USA, LLC

TOPCON AMERICA CORPORATION

COLOPHON

DESIGN

Melissa Kaup-Augustine, Lizard Press

TYPEFACE

Adobe Minion

SOFTWARE

Adobe Acrobat, Adobe Photoshop, LizardTech Genuine Fractals,
Markzware Flightcheck, Microsoft Word, QuarkXPress

HARDWARE

Macintosh computers, Nikon Super Coolscan 4000,
Epson Stylus Photo 1280

PRINTING/BINDING

InterPress Ltd., Hong Kong

FIRST EDITION

2,500 copies